PICTURE PERFECT POETRY

PICTURE PERFECT POETRY

An Anthology of Ekphrastic Nature Poetry For Students

Carol J. Labuzzetta

ISBN: 979-8-9861369-1-2
Northern Loon Press
Ogema, Wisconsin

DEDICATION

Picture Perfect Poetry: An Anthology of Ekphrastic Nature Poetry for Students is dedicated to my mother. She inspired and encouraged me to write. We shared a love of words, children's literature, and poetry. She passed away the day before the submissions opened for this anthology. It is to her memory, Janice Fritz, that I dedicate this book. I hope I've made her proud.

Table of Contents

FOREWORD

After becoming an indie author/publisher in 2021 with my first chapbook, I knew I wanted to pursue writing and publishing. My submissions to other online and print publications continued but were met with little success. At the same time, I realized many other authors in the poetry groups to which I belong, including Poetry Friday, also met some difficulty being published conventionally.

Recognizing our work was as good or better than that being accepted for publication, I decided to publish an anthology for children in middle grades. Since I am an environmental educator and often work writing into my lessons, the focus of the book was to be nature poetry.

In addition to being talented writers who deserved publication, many of the Poetry Friday group members are excellent photographers or at least enjoy photography, as I do. This is evident in our weekly round-up where new poetry is shared, often along with personal photographs.

Thus, I wanted to offer an opportunity to recognize both the poetry and photography talents of the people I read weekly and others who were interested. Some authors included in this book have been published many times, and this is the first publication for others.

There are many authors whose work deserves to be read. I wanted to acknowledge and share their work, as well as my own.

I discussed the idea for this book in the spring and summer of 2023 with my mother, deciding on the submission timeline, the book layout, and production periods. I was grateful to have her support for the project.

What Is Ekphrastic Poetry?

According to the Poetry Foundation, "ekphrastic poetry is a vivid description of a scene or, more commonly, a work of art." The word ekphrastic means "description" in Greek.

All of the poems in this book represent ekphrastic poetry. The works of art in this anthology are all photographs taken by the poets.

Authors and Photographers
Contributing to
Picture Perfect Poetry

Marcie Flinchum Atkins
Linda Baie
Schuyler Becker
Willeena Booker
Josie De Falco
Karen Eastlund
Joanne L. Emery
Patricia J.Franz
Molly Hogan
Tracy Kiff-Judson
Michelle Kogan
Denise R. Krebs
Carol J.Labuzzetta
Jone Rush MacCulloch
Linda Middleton
Kate McCarroll Moore
Colleen Murphy
Sally Murphy
Ian Rodrigues
Paula Schulz
Janice Scully
Joyce P. Uglow
Sandra Vaisnoras
Carol Varsalona
Alan j Wright

Photograph by Carol J. Labuzzetta

IN PRAISE OF DRAGONFLIES

Dragonfly swarms—

bursts with summer energy,

winds its way through the pond.

Each plant bows

folded in prayer—

especially the lotus.

Especially the lotus

folded in prayer

each plant bows,

winds its way through the pond,

bursts with summer energy—

dragonfly swarms.

Poem and photograph by
Marcie Flinchum Atkins

UPON WAKING IN A SUNFLOWER FIELD

Sun

beams

upon

sunflower—

daily alarm clock.

She waves back petal by petal.

Poem and photograph by
Marcie Flinchum Atkins

energized by sun
swallowtail welcomes each bloom—
summer's best friendships

Poem and photograph by
Marcie Flinchum Atkins

THINGS TO DO IF YOU ARE A SUNSET

Blush
Sneak in
Put on neon
Delight in feathered flight
Hopscotch from cloud to cloud
Inspect your reflection on water
Flash one last surprise
Dazzle
Fade

Poem and photograph by
Karen Eastlund

IF I WERE THE SKY

If I were the sky
On a windy day
Watching bare branches
Writhe and sway
I'd turn my back to the trees and say
"Would you please
You tallest of trees
Scratch my itches away?"

*Poem and photograph by
Karen Eastlund*

AUTUMN'S HOLD

Pumpkins squat and bright and round
Gathered now in autumn's hold
Your droll expressions so renowned
Pumpkins squat and bright and round.
What message in this fall playground?
Leave a seed! Shine your light! Be bold!
Pumpkins squat and bright and round
Gathered now in autumn's hold.

Poem and photograph by
Karen Eastlund

HEARTFUL

Heartful
Earth jade rose-tinged
Pads raised in modest praise
Prickly Pear holds my gaze
Giving hope-twinged
Peace pull

Poem and photograph by
Denise R. Krebs

GRANITE

Granite boulder waits
Unnoticed, highlighting her
Iron by rusting

Poem and photograph by
Denise R. Krebs

23

WARNING

Dying
After the fire
Nature called 911
Decades later repair's begun

Now fire
Becomes more dire
Climate change warns today
Will Joshua Trees go away?

Poem and photograph by
Denise R. Krebs

TO BE BOLD

On an autumn forest hillside,
A tree swaps green for gold,
As though that one among them
Decided to be bold.

Then the rest catch on,
Like colour's all the scene,
And every tree is rushing
To be anything but green.

Poem and photograph by
Ian Rodrigues

NATURE WALK

An overcast sky
Ruffled mushroom standing small
The endless wild green

Poem and photograph by
Schuyler Becker

HUNGRY BEAR LIMERICK

A bear on a mission to eat
broke into a house on my street.
In search of some breakfast,
he left quite a wreckfest,
one I fear he'll repeat.

*Poem and photograph by
Patricia J. Franz*

27

One too-slow-to-get-moving toad
tarrying in the wrong place.
One snake slithering
at a swift pace.
Lunge!
Grab!
Gulp!
So ends the chase.

Poem and photograph by
Molly Hogan

Photograph by Carol J. Labuzzetta

Photograph by Molly Hogan

BLACK-CROWNED NIGHT HERON

Stepping lightly along low tide's banks,
the young heron offers up
white dotted feathers, amber eyes,
a bicolored beak,
a flow
chart to identification.
The label of name securely
in place
creates a sense
of comfort,
of knowing.

It is so easy to forget
that a name is not an ending
but an invitation.

For even as the heron flies away
its patterned wings
unveil themselves
into something
larger.
Something
so much
more.

Poem by Molly Hogan

FOREST
A Kenning Poem

I celebrate you, ancient forest of trees
I feel such peace
In green spaces
Such as these.

I think of you as…
Life-sustainer
Carbon-drainer
Plant-nourisher
Air-sharer
Planet-carer
Shade-provider
Animal-shelterer
Shadow-spreader
Bird-protector
Health-detector
Biodiversity, natural serenity,
Providing for humanity
I walk beneath your giant trees
Your shade and shadow canopies
I thank you for this special place
This leafy strip, this silent space.

Poem and photograph by
Alan j Wright

Photograph by Alan j Wright

THE GARDEN, EARLY MORNING

To walk in the garden early
Before the sun
Owns the day
Delivers delight
To the curious wanderer.

The smells of the earth rise up
The last of the evening dew
Hangs on grateful leaves
The scent of lemon blossom
lingers in the air
As small creatures emerge
from hideouts
Resting places
and secret lairs
Bugs, beetles, butterflies.

Poem by Alan j Wright

RIDING THROUGH THE RAIN IN HANOI

Wet season downpour
plastic poncho protection
rain-ready cover
riding on through the cloudburst
this storm-resisting cyclist.

36   *Poem and photograph by Alan j Wright*

Photograph by Carol J. Labuzzetta

Photograph By Michelle Kogan

SUMMER SOLSTICE DISCOVERY

Sparkle summer jewel
spread your hungry
transforming warmth—
Perform your eating dance
day by day and
grow and grow—
Chrysalis yourself
and before you know
you'll metamorphosize
with marvelous gusto—
Mighty Monarch caterpillar.

Poem by
Michelle Kogan

SUNFLOWER

hip high september
sunflowers unfurl ready
treasures—birds delight.

*Poem and photograph by
Michelle Kogan*

Photograph by Carol Varsalona

Photograph by Michelle Kogan

NATURE AWAITS NOTICE…

Stalks
and leaves
sculpted by
wind, rain, and sun
create collages
of texture-tapestries,
botanical time capsules
capturing summertime snippets—
Sit-a-spell and soak in their grandeur…

Poem by
Michelle Kogan

Photo by Tracey Kiff-Judson

FIERY FRIEND

I know you from
tigers and tangerines,
carrots and parrots,
saffron and sunsets;

You mingle with
goldfish and marigolds,
campfires and cantaloupe,
corals and orioles,

but I did not expect
to find you in forests
dressed down as
commonplace
fungus.

Poem by Tracey Kiff-Judson

*Poem and photograph
by Tracey Kiff-Judson*

CANNIBAL SLUG

After the rain,
rolled out flat as a rug,
mashed by a car,
lies a goopy, squashed slug.

Here comes his friend
to console and to hug.
No!
She…
bites this poor dude
with her own slimy mug!

Who would have thought
she could be such a thug?
Eating her friend—
ugh, a cannibal slug!

CROCUS MAGIC

You're the lime sweetshop of lollipops,
silk collection cups for sundrops
and hints of heaven for waking bees,
sailing the starry dewdrop seas.

Goblets brimming blackberry juice
and saffron-spiced soft moonshine mousse,
around tall trunks you whirl and weave,
offering sweet sips to those who believe.

You're an army with spearlike shoots,
bold, brave before big welly boots.
From winter chill you softly tiptoe,
bringing sun-splashed lantern glow.

Poem and photograph by
Linda Middleton

47

Photograph by Linda Middleton

FLIGHT OF JEWELS

I call you a bright flight of jewels,
a glow of gems in dusted pools,
a celebration of spring, a dance of wings.

I call you iridescent day tripper,
sweet nectar sipper,
flower-to-flower flitter of opalescent glitter.

You are the summer flag waver,
lemon sunshine bather,
bluebell, betony and buddleia seeker,
the light flitter, the bright flutter,
a mesmerising eyespot peeker.

You are the clever dead leaf disguise
before the burst of magical surprise,
nature's treasure cycle keeper
and winter hideaway sleeper.

And as I'm drawn
into your whirlpool azure eyes,
I wish you would stay
and not flitter-flutter away…

Poem by
Linda Middleton

LEMONADE WAVE

Wild waves curl and crash
Bubbles refresh summer skies
Lemonade on rocks

Poem and photograph by
Linda Middleton

A HAIKU

sunflower peeks down
daisy looks up in wonder
a new friendship

Poem and photo by
Sandra Vaisnoras

Photo by Sandra Vaisnoras

EARTHY WORM

no limbs
no eyes
no wings to soar

ring-like tube
wrapped
in bristles
inches
forward
silently

eating
dead leaves
scraps of food
three times
its weight
each day

tunneling
burrowing
helping
Mother Earth
breathe

no one
notices
nature's
ecosystem
engineer

Lumbricus terrestris

Poem by Sandra Vaisnoras

JELLYFISH

It seems
you lack substance.
But that's
a clever ruse
you use
to make sure
you survive.
Perhaps you think
if no one sees you
no one will make waves
or ask anything of you.
That may be true
but I see your
gentle shimmer
and know
there is more to you
than meets the eye.

*Poem and photograph by
Sally Murphy*

HALF AWAKE

Half awake
or half asleep?
One eye closed,
the other open
in case of danger.
It might look strange
but it keeps you safe
whether you are
half awake
or half asleep.

Poem and photograph by
Sally Murphy

NOISY GUESTS

What's that ruckus
in my yard?
A feathered trio
laughing hard.

What's that rumpus
I can hear?
They're carolling
that rain is near.

What's that riot
on my fence?
Kookaburras
making sense!

Poem and photograph by
Sally Murphy

Photograph by Carol J. Labuzzetta

Photo by Joanne L. Emery

AUTUMN PLUNGE

I am here,
in this once-green place.
It is now dancing with
Autumn colors:
Red and orange swirl,
Yellow dazzles,
Brown and russet soothe.
I am here in the woods
wading into the fall unafraid.
Wind rustles the leaves,
birds chirp from branches,
water rushes over river stones.
I am here soaking it all up,
bathing in color-filled woods.
I dive between the trees:
maples, elms, oaks, and the white birches.
I glide up the path,
filling my mind with as much color
as it can hold.
I submerge myself in yellow,
In deep red, in bright orange.
Plunging headfirst into Autumn,
The trees take me over,
hold me and care for me.
Then ever so slowly, so slowly…
I return to the surface.
I am here peacefully floating,
resting in the arms of the woods.

Poem by
Joanne L. Emery

Photograph by Paula Schulz

SNAKE

Tines of my tongue eat each morning's light.

I join my brothers, the tall grasses,
in their hiss-whisper and sway-shake dance.

Today, as every day, I am tiled and terrific,
slipping through sunlight, an utterly clean jewel.

I am a pattern no basket weaver
can replicate and I am learning

to fit into my life as the mosaic
of my skin fits into itself, learning

to slip easily through the natural world.

Poem by Paula Schulz

LEAVE THE LEAVES ALONE
A Golden Shovel Poem

Lovers of the land **leave**

lush forest blankets where they fall. Wind rustles **the**

rich leafy litter calling attention to **leaves**

that feed life. Be wise—leave the leaves **alone.**

Poem and photograph by
Joyce P. Uglow

SUNDAY MORNING HAIKU

the way the light falls

on ordinary goodness

waiting to be shared

Poem and photograph by
Kate McCarroll Moore

MAINE MEDITATION

Be here,
on the water.
Breathe in blue…
Exhale.

Be here,
Surrounded
by evergreens.
Relax.

Be here,
in this wild place.
Feel the wind
Rejuvenate.

Be here.
Feel the rhythm
of the currents'
Flow…

Be here,
Mountains rising.
Lift your eyes.
Calm your spirits.

Poem and photograph by Joanne L. Emery 65

Photograph by Kate McCarroll Moore

REGENERATION

This used to be a tree

a forty-foot-tall redwood

planted on a backyard hillside, shading the house

a place for birds and squirrels—

oxygen and dappled sunlight mingled

there for decades, a quiet life

Wild winter storms swept in,

skytears falling for days on days

till roots un-rooted, tall tree

untethered, began its perilous tilt

Sodden sorrow, down it came

stump of redwood, all that remained

A season later, tree grows still

fairy haven on the hill

lights are on, somebody's home

wildlife, new life, welcome sign

sun and nature's green design

Poem by Kate McCarroll Moore

A DAISY'S DISCOURSE

A Weed?
Indeed!
Who says it's so?
Who dictates where we ought to grow?
We've been around for scores and scores,
been trampled by the dinosaurs.
Throughout the world, we represent
on almost every continent.
And yet, you say, we're out of place?
I disagree; we've earned our space.

A Weed?
Indeed!
Whose point of view?
The bees aren't in accord with you.
When given room, our lot displays
a throng of nectar-filled bouquets,
because on every daisy's head
a hundred flowers fill its bed.
Instead of urging us to go,
the bees encourage us to grow.

A Weed?
Indeed!
We're well aligned
with flowers' traits, as they're defined.
For evidence, let me relay,
we've colored florets, disc and ray.
We've everything a structure needs
to reproduce, develop seeds.
We meet the features through and through.
Ask Webster; he'll proclaim it's true.

To those in doubt, rethink your thought.
A weed?
Indeed!
We're clearly not.

Poem and photograph by
Colleen Murphy

Poem and photograph by
Colleen Murphy

IT'S ONLY NATURAL
The Case of Photosynthesis

Once within a maple leaf
the Pigment children grew.
The foursome feuded frequently,
as siblings often do.

"If only you could share the light
and not be such a meanie,"
Goldie, Red, and Ginger each,
would often say to Greenie.
"You're like a blanket over us
who's taking all our sun.
How'd that even happen?
You're outnumbered three to one!"

"What can I say?" asked Greenie.
"It's a critical attraction.
It's not my fault I'm gifted
with this chemical reaction.
You ought to be appreciative
instead of always rude,
since I'm the one among us
who produces all our food."

"See, there you go," said Ginger,
"with you thinking we're below you."
"That's right," said Red and Goldie.
"You just wait and we will show you."

When Autumn shortened summer's days
and Greenie disappeared,
it took the siblings by surprise,
but then those children cheered.
"At last," they said, "the world will see
the splendor of us all!"
But little did the trio know
how quickly they would fall.

FAIRYTALE FUNGI

Along the woodland trail
There is magic for you to see,
Sprouting from a tree stump
Under the leafy canopy.

Clusters of fairy bonnets
Glisten in the morning dew,
Like bell-shaped umbrellas
Pale grey and honey hue.

Dainty as a thimble,
The trooping crumble caps,
A well-suited nickname
For these fragile chaps.

Rose-tinted lamellae
With a velvety-soft texture,
A perfect hat for fairykind,
Take comfort and shelter.

Poem and photograph by
Josie De Falco

*Photograph by
Josie De Falco*

THE WILD GOOSE

I ruffle my grey feathers,
Stretch out my long neck.
Watch the people go by
Along a wooden deck.

Envious of their voyage,
Sailboats out to sea.
Can I come with you?
I wish to be free.

Craving the salty sea air
Waddling down to the
shore,
My thirst for adventure
I can no longer ignore.

I know I should stay
Together with our flock,
But I want so much more
Than life on this rock.

My dreams of gliding
Over rocky mountains
Follow the seaplanes
To paradise islands.

A voice is calling me.
Is it the wind I can hear?
Spread out your wings
There's nothing to fear.

Poem by Josie De Falco

A HAIRY VISITOR

Beside the garden bucket
An unexpected visitor
Wiggles across a rose leaf,
A tiny hairy creature.

Is it a little tiger
Who prowls in a leafy jungle
With fur of flaming fire?
After much deliberation
I'm still none the wiser.
What could it be?

"A sycamore moth caterpillar,"
My granny tells me.

Snowy-white sequins are
Embroidered along its back.
My curiosity deepens.
Should it not be
On a sycamore tree?

"It's finding a place to pupate,"
My granny tells me.

Our newfound friend,
We hope to see you soon
In the garden of mid-June,
Hatched from a silk cocoon.

Poem and Photograph by
Josie De Falco

NAMING THE WORLD

James, at two, is so sure of the world.
Look at the tomatoes, I tell him,
pointing to the potted plant on the patio,
laden with green fruit,
a week away from ripening.

Those are apples, he tells me.
He wraps his hand around one gently,
leans in closer to check.
They look like apples, I tell him,
but they are tomatoes.
Soon they'll be
juicy, ripe, and red,
and we can eat them.
No, he says—they're apples.

Who am I to argue?

Poem and photograph by Kate McCarroll Moore

MOON GLOW

Moon
you pose,
greeting me
at eveningtide.
I stare surprised by
your glowing appearance
and regal statuesque stance.
You're not the old man in the moon
But a friendly face guiding me home.

Poem and photograph
by Carol Varsalona

Photograph by Carol Varsalona

AUTUMN ADVENTURE

We wind around the bend
and what do we see?
Rows of pumpkins
as orange as can be.

Off the hayride we jump
with excited delight
searching for a pumpkin
that will shine with a light.

What an Autumn surprise
on an October day
finding nature's bounty
in a picturesque way.

Poem by Carol Varsalona

AUTUMN'S BEAUTY

nature's canopy
gracefully scatters leaves
splendiferous fall

Poem and photograph by Carol Varsalona

ALONE

puddle pockets pass by
and I keep treading,
determined to keep afloat.
though the ripples
tip and toss my presence.
Side to side,
on the inside,
love lifts me
out of the deep dark
and I dare to dance
on the water like light
lingering its reflection
on me

Poem and photograph by
Willeena Booker

83

Photograph by Willeena Booker

TOGETHER

Outward light lingers long,
beckons both
being in need
of the other,

forever foraging forward
with whimsical wishes
pushing past leaf and
stone, stem steep
while sunbeams seed the way

ascending up
to the sweet spot,
saturated in peace,
gleaning goodness and strength

the nectar is life
sustaining, each living thing
busy basking in the beauty of the
other

Poem by Willeena Booker

MY DEAR,

Be a dear,
Be quick to sound the alarm
Whenever there is trouble
Be the first to do no harm
Be quick to protect
Be of a warm affect
Be observant
Across the verdant
landscape
Be slow to react
But quick to respond
Be the first to arrive
To show love
Out into the unknown
Oh Dear, watch that love
boomerang

Poem and photograph by Willeena Booker

MELANCHOLY AIR

These boots that
laced up the memories
of kinship with mountain trails,
and those who hiked
along with me,
sit idly waiting
for those feet to fill them
one more time.

Poem and photograph by
Linda Baie

HUMANS LEARN BUT OFTEN DON'T

a tiny space
of woven lace
carries a spider's
deadly embrace

that need for a meal
no human appeal
only nature's zeal
for constructing steel

it isn't news
it's nature's blues
humans choose
opposing views

Poem and photograph by
Linda Baie

©jone rush macculloch

Photograph by
Jone Rush MacCulloch

WHEN A SEEDLING DOES YOGA

Roots threading
inhale

Taproots burrowing
exhale

Stems pushing
grounded in mountain pose

Sun-kissed branches
stretching in warrior pose

One day, on my stomach in sphinx pose
I will read under your shade

Inhale, exhale
Namaste

Poem by
Jone Rush MacCulloch

AUTUMN CONFETTI

Every leaf speaks to me fluttering
from the autumn tree.

—Emily Brönte

I sit by the river **every**

fall, watching each **leaf**

change crimson, amber, and rust. The wind **speaks**

inviting the leaves **to**

sail, scatter, let go of now. Reminding **me**

of children swirling, twirling, and **fluttering**

in the forest away **from**

the world and its chaos. **The**

leaves know **autumn**

dancing, spiraling from the **tree**

Poem and Photograph by
Jone Rush MacCulloch

A ZEN GARDEN IN GOLDEN GATE PARK

Tucked
away.
Inspired
by Chinese stone
landscapes brought by monks
to Japan long ago—
boulders symbolize mountains,
gravel resembles ocean waves.
Shhh. Listen. Feel the silent rhythm.

Poem and photograph by
Janice Scully

AN AFTERNOON NAP

What a comfy pillow
comrades make,

when my belly is full of
squid and hake.

Snoozing on
this slippery bed,

with clouds and seagulls
overhead.

Poem and photograph by
Janice Scully

95

SPRING VISITOR

you stand, stare
a mama's steel eyes
nose lifts, sniffs

danger

teddy-round ears, so cute
cinnamon-spring coat…**WAIT!**

96

Go! Scram!
*ladle-to-pot-**CLANGGG! CLANGGG!***

This is my home!

you
barely blink

my babies are here
their tree
quiet forest spot
we will stay

this is our home

Poem and photograph by
Patricia J. Franz

CALIFORNIA CORMORANTS

Catching their breath
on this rocky ledge

after hunting for lunch
on this coastal edge.

Miraculous divers!
Rugged wings and webbed feet

plunge into the surf
when they need a fish treat.

*Poem and photograph by
Janice Scully*

LEOPARD FROG

Mossy leopard frog

Hiding near the water's edge

So still and quiet

Until footsteps approach you

Jump! Splash! Off you go to swim!

Poem and photograph by
Carol J. Labuzzetta

A GHOSTLY NONET

White
Ghost pipe
Colorless
Forest dweller
Chlorophyll-less plant
A fun find in damp woods
Confused often with mushrooms
Monotropa uniflora
Droopy flower heads not quite ready

Poem and photograph by
Carol J. Labuzzetta

Four Fabulous
Funky Forest Fungi
Found Friday
Foraging For Food

Poem and photograph by
Carol J. Labuzzetta

Photograph by
Joyce P. Uglow

TREEFROG
A Mesostic Poem

Your green moTtling hides

you from your suRroundings.

You're greenest whEn hopping

around near the pond's Edges of

Forest's trees.

Does it huRt to stick your toe pads

to branches of Oak and on the scrubby shrubs?

Maybe you like my Grubby hand best!

Poem by
Joyce P. Uglow

Photograph by Tracey Kiff-Judson

IVY DRIVING

Lacey raced her flat-bed Chevy,
blasting through this country town,
gassing, running, grinding, gunning
hard until its parts broke down.

Lacey drove her beat-up Chevy
to a field of sunburned hay,
chugging,
        choking,
            coasting,
                smoking...
Lacey left it to decay.

Now who's driving this old Chevy?
Ivy climbs in, creeps around,
twisting, hugging, coaxing, tugging
into slow-digesting ground.

Poem by
Tracey Kiff-Judson

Index of Poems Found in this Book

Poetry Resources

For the classroom teacher, homeschool leader, or independent student work.

This book can be used as a mentor text for teaching poetry in the classroom. All of the poetry contained within the book is ekphrastic poetry.

Several additional photographs are provided as page breaks from which students can try writing an ekphrastic poem of their own.

Responding with poetry to the image is the first step, but thereafter, a student might want to try writing one of the specific types of poetry listed above. For those types, resources are provided in this section for the student and teacher to enhance their understanding of how the poem should be structured.

Alliteration
Alliteration is a literary device found in poems or is a poem itself. It is the repetitive use of the first sound in a series of words. It can be used to give a poem a pulse or beat or add a lyrical element.

Students might be familiar with alliteration made famous as "tongue twisters." It can be used to bring attention to a subject or product. There are many examples of alliteration in pop culture. Can you name some?

Sources: Poetry4Kids.com, PoetryFoundation.org, literaryterms.net/ alliteration

Ekphrastic Poetry
Ekphrastic poetry is defined in the foreword section of this book. All poems in this book are examples of ekphrastic poetry.

Fib
Many students are familiar with the mathematical pattern called the Fibonacci sequence. Are you familiar with it? The Fib poem takes the sequence of numbers found in Fibonacci's pattern and uses it as a starting point for syllable counts in each line of the poem for twenty syllables in all. This six-line poetic form was created by Gregory Pincus in 2006.

For example, the sequence 1, 1, 2, 3, 5, 8 . . . results by adding the two previous numbers together to get the next number in the sequence. This results in a poem of twenty total syllables. The first line has one syllable, the second line has one syllable, the third line has two syllables, the fourth line, three syllables, and so on.

Only a cursory understanding of the Fibonacci sequence is necessary to write a poem using the pattern. I think this would be a fun integrated math–language arts project. Are you willing to try it?

Source: writersdigest.com

Free Verse Poem

Free verse poems have no form requirements with rhyming, meter, or formatting patterns. This type of poem can be difficult because the word choice becomes significantly important in the conveyance of what the author wants to be read—be that an object, emotion, or an event.

According to Nesbitt, literary techniques such as alliteration, personification, unique formatting, or onomatopoeia are employed by the poet to help convey meaning as well.

Golden Shovel

A Golden Shovel is a type of poem that uses a line from a poem you like to write another poem in which each of your lines ends with the words in order of the line you selected. The poem of the original line or quote is credited to that author. If you choose a poem or quote with five words, then your new poem will be five lines long.

The subject of your poem can differ from the line you used. Perhaps the best way to understand how a Golden Shovel poem works is to read one. There are two Golden Shovel poems in this book. Can you find them?

Source: writersdigest.com

Haiku

Haiku is an ancient form of Japanese poetry that focuses on nature. Traditional haiku have a rhyme scheme of 5 syllables–7 syllables–5 syllables. The first and last lines have five syllables and the middle line has seven.

Haiku, being highly descriptive with just a few words, should evoke an image in the reader's mind.

Tips on writing haiku:
- Do not write complete sentences.
- Be sure to sound out your syllables if you want to write a traditional haiku.
- Use a dictionary if you are unsure of the syllable count in a word (this is a great exercise for elementary-aged students).
- Get rid of any connecting words (is, and, but, then, the, etc.).
- The third line of the haiku should add a twist or surprise observation (this is often left unaddressed by even experienced writers of this type of poetry).

Modern (Americanized) haiku often have fewer than seventeen syllables and can be written in one continuous line instead of three broken ones. There is a modern haiku in this book. Can you find it?

Haiku seem simple and fun. However, they are also difficult to master as they require more specific requirements than just the syllable count. You can refer to *www.haiku-poetry.org/what-is-haiku.html* for more information.

School-aged children enjoy this style of poetry, as it does not (and should not) rhyme!

Kenning poem

The kenning poem is another form of ancient poetry! Who knew poetry has been written for so many centuries?

Kenning poems use words (usually in pairs of two) to describe something without using its name. These poems often start by listing attributes and actions of your subject and then creating alternative word descriptors.

Kenning poems create a new view of something familiar by describing it in imaginative ways. For example: an airplane might become a sky-glider, or a clam might be a pearl-keeper.

Kenning poems might also be presented to the reader as a puzzle to figure out, asking "What am I writing about here?"

Source: Poetry4kids.com

Limerick

My first introduction to this popular form of poetry was my mother. From her teaching days she left a body of work, including some limericks.

Like haiku, tanka, nonets, and other poetic forms, limericks have a set of "rules" to follow. These rules include:
- a rhyme scheme of AABBA
- five lines
- a distinctive rhythm or beat
- humor
- a first line that ends with a person's name (usually)
- a funny last line.

Ken Nesbitt's website, *Poetry4Kids.com*, offers the above rules as well as downloadable worksheets for your students on this popular type of poetry.

Mesostic Poem

A mesostic poem is similar to an acrostic poem, but instead of using the word vertically on the left edge to start each line, the mesostic poem has a word or phrase that runs down the middle of the poem, contained within the line. The word is indicated by the use of capital letters.

Acrostic poems are fun, with a word, phrase, or name spelled out vertically down one of the edges; usually, the left edge, used for the theme of the poem.

Mesostic poems present more of a challenge for the student or poet looking for one.

Source: digitalsalon.com

Nonet

Nonets consist of nine lines with a descending order of syllables, starting with nine. The first line is followed by a line of eight syllables, then seven, six, five, four, three, two, and finally ends with a one-syllable line. It is a simple yet fun type of poetry.

A reverse nonet simply reverses the order of the lines of syllables; the poem starts with a one-syllable line and ends with a line of nine syllables.

Source: writersdigest.com

Reverso
This type of poem was invented by a teacher-poet named Marilyn Singer. It would be a good exercise with wordplay for middle-school students. You can read more about it on Singer's website at *www.readbrightly.com/reverso.*

In brief, a reverso is a poem with two halves. The second half reverses the lines from the first half in exact order, with only changes in punctuation and capitalization. The result is entirely different than what is written in the first half of the poem.

A reverso poem can be difficult to write. What do you think? Are you up to the challenge?

Shape or Concrete Poem
Several poems in this book are examples of shape poems. A shape poem is when the words are arranged in a specific way to reveal a shape. It can also be referred to as concrete poetry.

Shape poems can present a challenge for publishers but can be great fun in the classroom. Ken Nesbitt offers instructions on how to construct a shape poem on his website, P*oetry4kids.com.*

Tanka
A tanka poem uses a similar yet longer form of syllabic verse when compared to haiku. The word tanka refers to a short song and is considered a modern English form of poetry.

Its structure follows a syllable line pattern of 5-7-5-7-7 for a total of thirty-one syllables as opposed to seventeen total syllables of a haiku.

There are a few more "rules."
- Tanka has no punctuation or rhyming words.
- Vivid imagery is used, consisting of powerful words.
- A short story is told.

Source: Poetry4Kids.com

Triolet
According to Ken Nesbitt, this poetic format hails from 13th-century France and contains repeated lines.

It has eight total lines with a rhyme scheme of ABaAabAB. A and B signify the repeated lines, which means when you write a triolet there are a limited number of new lines one has to create.

Again, this form of poetry might be easier to understand by reading an example of it. There is an example of a triolet in this book.

Another way to look at the repeated lines is that lines 1, 4, and 7 are the same (represented by A). Lines 2 and 8 are the same, represented by B. The lowercase a and b rhyme with the uppercase lines of the same letter but are not repeated.

Clear and mud, right? Go to page 21 to see for yourself! You can do it!

Sources: Poetry4Kids.com and writersdigest.com

Tip on syllable counting

Use a dictionary to help with syllable counts! When I led a writer's circle for third-grade students, I found they were unfamiliar with all the ways a dictionary could assist them in word choice and confirming a syllable count.

We get sloppy in our speech and diction is relaxed enough to not allow our ears to hear each syllable. I used the following example: How many syllables are in the word Niagara?

It was rare that a student could identify the four syllables in the word Niagara.

Additional Resources

Alliteration
https://www.poetryfoundation.org/learn/glossary-terms/alliteration

Ekphrastic poetry
https://www.poetryfoundation.org/learn/glossary-terms/ekphrasis

https://www.readwritethink.org/classroom-resources/lesson-plans/ekphrasis-using-inspire-poetry

Golden Shovel
https://www.writersdigest.com/write-better-poetry/golden-shovel-poetic-form

Haiku Poetry: Experiencing Life in 5-7-5
https://www.haiku-poetry.org/what-is-haiku.html

Mesostic
https://www.digitalsalon.com/acrostics-mesostics-and-double-acrostics

Nonet
https://www.writersdigest.com/write-better-poetry/nonet-poems-poetic-form

Triolet
https://www.writersdigest.com/personal-updates/triolet-an-easy-way-to-write-8-lines-of-poetry

Reverso
https://www.readbrightly.com/reverso-poetry-writing-verse-reverse/

Your Turn

Are you ready to try ekphrastic poetry? The photographs on the following pages offer a chance for you or your students to write a descriptive poem in response to the photograph they choose. Even though all the poems in this book represent ekphrastic poetry, the authors chose different forms. There is a wide choice for variation.

Pages: 13, 29, 37, 41, and 57.

Acknowledgments

With this book comes the need to thank many people. Firstly, I'd like to thank all the author-photographers who contributed to Picture Perfect Poetry. They trusted me with their work, and for that I am eternally grateful. I want to thank the book's editor, Rachel Reyes, who spent hours of her time relentlessly going over the language and grammar used in the poems and my formatting. Lastly, I want to thank my husband and sons who are always encouraging me, no matter what I choose to do.

9 7 9 8 9 8 6 1 3 6 9 1 2